CREATIVE CAREERS

Creative Careers in MUSIC

Terri Dougherty

San Diego, CA

For more information, contact:
ReferencePoint Press, Inc.
PO Box 27779
San Diego, CA 92198
www.ReferencePointPress.com

LIBRARY OF CONGRESS CATALOGING-IN-PUBLICATION DATA

Names: Dougherty, Terri, author.
Title: Creative careers in music / by Terri Dougherty.
Description: San Diego, CA : ReferencePoint Press, 2025. | Series: Creative careers | Includes bibliographical references and index.
Identifiers: LCCN 2025004650 (print) | LCCN 2025004651 (ebook) | ISBN 9781678210281 (library binding) | ISBN 9781678210298 (ebook)
Subjects: LCSH: Music trade--Vocational guidance--Juvenile literature.
Classification: LCC ML3795 .D68 2025 (print) | LCC ML3795 (ebook) | DDC 780.23--dc23/eng/20250205
LC record available at https://lccn.loc.gov/2025004650
LC ebook record available at https://lccn.loc.gov/2025004651

Contents

Introduction: Pursuing a Creative Career in Music

As a high school student, Jillissa Anderson believed a career in music followed one of two main paths: education or performance. "Little did I know there was a whole world of musical career options,"[1] says Anderson. Opportunities for a career in music are wide, varied, and sometimes surprising. From a career as a music producer, manager, or sound engineer, to a job as a DJ, instrument repair technician, or forensic musicologist, an interest in music can take you in a multitude of creative directions. Anderson has worked in a variety of jobs and is a clarinet specialist at a music store in addition to being a performer and teacher.

Anderson's experience demonstrates that not all who work in the field of music are destined to be onstage. Even in the realm of musical performance, there are many jobs behind the scenes that are just as fulfilling. Sound technicians make sure a musical performer's efforts reach an audience's ears, while music producers have the ultimate control over a song when they combine vocal, instrument, and beat tracks. Popular singers and music groups have a team of professionals who contribute to their success, including a manager, booking agent, lawyer, and accountant, as well as marketing and social media specialists. Louise Lelièvre knew she wanted to work in the music industry after attending her first music festival at age sixteen. She now works in Montreal as communications manager at Groover, which gives artists feedback on their music and helps them gain visibility through playlist placements and social media shares. "Helping independent artists shape their career is my daily motivation,"[2] she comments.

Music and More

Combining other educational fields with an interest in music can also lead to a fascinating career. Knowledge of both music and business, for example, might lead to a job as an agent, manager, music marketer, or concert venue manager. A music lawyer could specialize in contract negotiations, intellectual property suits, or copyright cases. A forensic musicologist provides expert testimony in court cases, such as those involving copyright infringement, when knowledge of music theory and analysis is helpful and relevant.

Unexpected Paths to a Satisfying Career

Opportunities in the music field are wide ranging and can lead to exciting and creative careers, sometimes in unexpected ways. Michelle Cann, who is on the piano faculty at the Curtis Institute of Music, thought at one time that she wanted to concentrate on piano performance. She found a new path after becoming a choir director in an after-school program. "I realized I need to be doing things for people and with people,"[3] she reflects. She began working as a church choir director, started her own studio, and is also a soloist and chamber musician.

Some people like Cann forge new paths to fulfilling careers; others periodically reassess their talents, opportunities, and desires to find satisfying outlets for their love of music. During her diversified music career, drummer Alana Velvis has taught music students, scheduled lessons for other teachers and students, and toured with tribute bands. Now the owner of a music café, she appreciates the way she has been able to juggle and rework things to keep music in her life. "The trick is to figure out how it's going to work for you and what you want out of it," she reflects. "One of my strengths is to always be reevaluating."[4]

Performing and songwriting are high-profile careers that do happen for some. Country singer and songwriter Megan Moroney, who gained success with the song “Tennessee Orange,” wrote her first song while a student at the University of Georgia. This earned her the opportunity to open for country singer Chase Rice, and that got her hooked on performing. She switched her college major from accounting to marketing and music business and interned with country singer Kristian Bush’s music publishing company in Nashville. She began working with Bush, who is half of the country duo Sugarland, and he produced her first albums. Her career continued to rise when she won the Country Music Association’s award for new artist of the year in 2024.

Success like Moroney’s is the exception rather than the rule in the music industry, but talent like hers is far from the only way to put an interest in music to work. There are many creative ways to turn musical interests into a career that strikes the right chord.

Music Therapist

What Does a Music Therapist Do?

When a toddler began panicking during a medical procedure, Elaine Kong was there to comfort and calm her. The music therapist began singing one of the child's favorite songs, and the toddler settled down so the medical team could complete an echocardiogram, which uses sound waves to get an image of the heart. Thanks to Kong's involvement, the team did not need to give the child extra medication to complete the procedure.

That same day Rosemary Obi, Kong's coworker and fellow music therapist at Golisano Children's Hospital in Rochester, New York, visited a teen who was coping with the eating disorder anorexia nervosa. Obi helped the patient learn to use music to ease anxiety. They worked through breathing and muscle relaxation techniques combined with music and later used music during an art activity. Obi also proposed that the teen create a soundtrack for her life to help her express herself in a new and meaningful way.

Music therapists like Obi and Kong combine the healing power of music with knowledge of therapy to help patients overcome physical

At a Glance

Number of Jobs
19,200 in 2023

Pay
About $50,558 in 2023

Educational Requirements
Bachelor's degree

Personal Qualities
Good communicator and listener, critical thinker, service oriented, problem solver, reasoning skills, musical ability

Working Conditions
Hospital, office, school, nursing home

Future Job Outlook
Growth of 4 percent through 2028

and mental challenges. Music supports positive emotions, and music therapists use it to help clients alleviate depression, ease anxiety, and support well-being. “Most music therapists are accomplished musicians and have an interest in helping people empower themselves,”[5] says Jane Creagan, the director of professional programs for the American Music Therapy Association.

Working as a music therapist is different from being a performing musician or music teacher, notes Mai Abe, a board-certified music therapist and founder of Creative Vibes Music Therapy in the San Francisco Bay Area. While music therapists may perform for patients or teach them to use instruments to express themselves, those activities are part of a larger care plan designed to enhance a patient’s physical abilities and mental health. The music is chosen purposefully, Abe explains, and is used to work toward the therapist’s goals for a patient.

How Do You Become a Music Therapist?

Education and Training

Music therapists must have a bachelor’s degree in music therapy. This is typically a four-year degree that involves learning musical techniques and theory and studying psychology, human behavior, and treatment of behavioral disorders. Classes may include conducting, composition, music history, piano, guitar, and voice, as well as principles of therapy, human development, and psychology of music. Students also take general education courses in English, math, and social sciences.

Board-certified music therapists must complete a degree program in music therapy that includes twelve hundred hours of fieldwork in a college degree program. Fieldwork at a patient facility, for example, which is completed alongside the required coursework, allows students to learn how to assess a client’s needs, develop and implement treatment plans, and document the patient’s progress. Additional experience may be gained by

Enhancing the Power of Music

"The beauty of music is that it is inherently therapeutic even without intentionally setting goals. However, a music therapist can maximize all the benefits music provides. . . . We are able to identify and respond to different psychological conditions using music experiences."

—Mai Abe, music therapist

Quoted in CreativeVibesMT, *The Difference Between a Music Therapist, Teacher, and Musician: Music Therapy Advocacy and Education*, YouTube, January 5, 2023. www.youtube.com/watch?v=DMgVEq7BxGU.

volunteering in a nursing home, at a summer camp, or with another organization where people receive care and assistance.

Certified music therapists must pass an exam from the Certification Board for Music Therapists. A student who passes the certification exam becomes credentialed as a Music Therapist-Board Certified. The board certification must be renewed every five years. To renew their credentials, music therapists must continue to earn education credits and adhere to professional standards.

Those who already have a bachelor's degree in music or a related field can become a music therapist by taking courses in a certificate or master's degree program in music therapy. Abe has a bachelor's degree in clarinet performance from the Eastman School of Music and a master's degree in music therapy from Loyola University New Orleans.

Skills and Personality

People considering music therapy as a career should be empathetic as well as musical, because music therapists care about the patients they work with and understand how music can be used in treatment. Communication skills are also critical, since music therapists talk with patients and their families and other caregivers about sensitive and challenging situations. They ac-

Music therapists work with both children and adults. They combine the healing power of music with knowledge of therapy to help patients overcome a variety of physical and mental challenges.

tively listen to a patient's comments, asking appropriate questions when necessary. They write reports and analyze information presented to them by other members of the care team.

Other important skills include social perceptiveness. This requires being sensitive to how a patient reacts to a song or piece of music and recognizing when an issue arises. Creativity and critical thinking are used when considering how to solve a problem, weighing the pros and cons of alternatives, and creating a plan for moving forward. Crafting a treatment plan requires good judgment, reasoning, and decision-making skills, especially when music therapists are determining whether a treatment is working. They need to be versatile and adjust when circumstances change. "We utilize all aspects of music, whether it's creating, listening, discussing, or engaging, and we're constantly reassessing throughout the session to make sure the goals we've set are being met," Abe explains. "We have the training to redirect and change direction if need be."[6]

On the Job

Working with Patients

On any given day, a music therapist will develop a treatment plan for a patient and use music therapy to build rapport, provide emotional support, and help patients reach treatment goals. Each day Obi and Kong work with patients, supervise student interns, attend team rounds with other medical professionals, and write notes on patients' progress and all aspects of each treatment plan. They provide music therapy to patients who are dealing with a variety of health concerns, including cancer, eating disorders, blood disorders, heart disease, and other—often serious—conditions.

Abe has provided therapy to adults and teens in mental health and substance use disorder treatment as well as seniors in assisted living and memory care facilities. She has also worked with children and adults with intellectual or developmental disabilities. To relax patients or help them through difficult times, she employs a variety of musical practices, from songwriting to jamming to re-creating familiar songs with pleasant associations.

Music therapists may have their own practice or may work for a music therapy clinic. They may travel to a day care, senior center, or another setting to meet with clients. Abe has led several groups in assisted living homes and memory care units. Her first visit involves an assessment to gauge the personalities, dynamics, and musical tastes of the group she will be working with. "This allows me to formulate some goals and objectives for future sessions,"[7] Abe says. She chooses music and may even bring in instruments based on this information, but she is also flexible enough to respond to client needs in the moment.

After working with a patient, a music therapist evaluates the patient's progress and response to therapy and prepares a report. Music therapists collaborate with other health care professionals, communicating with them regarding the patient's condition. Obi's

A Job with Rewards

"Music therapy is an exciting and rewarding health care profession that is really continuing to grow. I have enjoyed being a music therapist and I feel fortunate that I have had the opportunity to make a difference in the lives of others."

—Jane Creagan, music therapist

Jane Creagan, "Career Options," American Music Therapy Association. https://musictherapy-assets-new.azureedge.net.

day typically ends at 5:30 p.m. after writing observations and recommendations on a patient's chart and reviewing the notes of her interns and other caregivers. Some nights she stays until after 6:00 p.m. "No day is the same," she says. "It's always interesting and I am always learning. And, most importantly, it's such a gift to bring music into our patients' and their families' lives and do it in a therapeutic way."[8]

Work Settings

A music therapist might be part of the staff at a general hospital, psychiatric hospital, rehabilitation facility, hospice, nursing home, or school. A music therapist could also work for a substance abuse program, day care facility, community program, oncology treatment center, or pain management clinic.

Some work full time for these institutions; others might be part-time therapists and have a second job as a musician or music teacher. Many continue to go to school to get a master's degree or doctorate in hopes of advancing their career. An additional degree in counseling or therapy can also be beneficial. "That will definitely make you far more marketable and valuable in the workforce,"[9] Abe says.

What Is the Future Outlook for Music Therapists?

The job outlook for music therapists is good. Job search website Zippia expects a job growth rate of 4 percent by 2028. CareerExplorer, an online platform that provides career information, also sees a generally positive job outlook for music therapists. It notes that research showing music's impact on brain stimulation supports acceptance of the career and projects a growth rate of 6.8 percent by 2026.

The average salary for music therapists in 2023 was $50,558, according to CareerExplorer. The lowest paid made $33,600 per year, while top-level music therapists made an average of $76,100. Chelsea Waddelow, a music therapy adjunct professor at Meredith College, comments on the Zippia site that music therapists in administrative and academic positions may earn higher salaries than those who work in clinical jobs.

Music therapists may need to advocate for their profession to show clients that the value of the services they provide goes beyond entertainment. As Obi is carrying her instrument tote of shakers, tambourines, drums, and more to see a three-year-old with appendicitis, she is sometimes asked whether she is going to give a concert. "That kind of well-meaning comment actually gives us a chance to clear up a misunderstanding of our role and let people know that we are not entertainers," Obi says. "We are highly trained board-certified music therapists who are part of our patients' treatment team."[10]

Find Out More

American Counseling Association

www.counseling.org

The website of the American Counseling Association explains what counseling is and what it is like to work with a counselor. It also has a section featuring interviews with counselors who describe their jobs in the mental health field. A search for music therapy brings up articles about creative art therapies, including music therapy.

American Music Therapy Association

www.musictherapy.org

This organization supports the music therapy profession through education, training, professional standards, and research. Its website provides information about a music therapy career, including professional qualifications and educational requirements. A directory lists schools offering music therapy degree programs.

Careers in Music

www.careersinmusic.com

This website features an overview of music-related careers, including music therapist. In addition to outlining the work of a music therapist, the site includes salary, career path, and education information.

Creative Vibes Music Therapy

www.creativevibesmt.com

The website of the Creative Vibes Music Therapy team includes blog posts that describe the benefits of music therapy techniques. The blog posts also show how music therapy is used in various settings.

What Does a Musician Do?

Playing bass guitar made Bryan Boliver's fingers ache, so he gave up and put the guitar under his bed. Then he heard the song "Brain Stew" by Green Day. "It's a very simple song to play," says Boliver. "I pulled the bass out from under my bed and started playing along with the song and I realized wow, if I can play along with this band then . . . the world literally opened up in that moment and honestly I've been playing ever since."[11] Boliver played in numerous bands with friends, learned to record the songs he wrote, and founded a music production company.

In her role as concertmaster of the National Symphony Orchestra in Washington, DC, violinist Nurit Bar-Josef is intimately familiar with the orchestra's concert music. She expertly performs her solos and marks music so string players move their bows in unison. If something is not going quite right during a rehearsal, a musician from another section will ask for her opinion. As a leader in the orchestra, she works closely with the conductor and leads musicians in tuning their instruments before a concert. "It's a combination of being both a soloist and a team player,"[12] she explains.

At a Glance

Number of Jobs
173,500

Pay
$52,379 in 2025

Educational Requirements
None

Personal Qualities
Musical talent, knowledge of musical techniques, interpersonal skills, perseverance

Working Conditions
Practice studio, recording studio, event, festival, concert hall

Future Job Outlook
Growth of 1.2 percent through 2032

Intense Preparation

"When we get a season announcement or when we get the draft of what is probably going to happen the following season I'm already in my head thinking, well . . . there are the Beethoven symphonies, I've played those several times, I know I won't need as much time preparing for those. But if it's something more obscure or if they're pieces that come up that we don't play all that often my preparation definitely starts months in advance, sometimes up to three months in advance."

—Nurit Bar-Josef, violinist and concertmaster of the National Symphony Orchestra in Washington, DC

Quoted in WETA Classical, "What Is a Concertmaster in an Orchestra? Nurit Bar-Josef of the NSO Explains," *Classical Breakdown*, YouTube, July 18, 2023. www.youtube.com/watch?v=MHtqKtiuD3s.

Whether they perform as a solo artist or as part of a band, orchestra, ensemble, or other group, musicians use their talent to spark emotion in those who hear the music they make. Their skill at playing an instrument or singing can set the mood, stir feelings, provide inspiration, deliver enjoyment, tell a story, and inspire thoughtful contemplation. Musicians have fun playing with others and connecting with their listeners. For casual or amateur performers, music may be a hobby or part-time gig, but some have made music their career and their primary source of income.

How Do You Become a Musician?

Education and Training

Musicians must be experts at playing one or more musical instruments, and this requires a great deal of training, talent, and practice. Training often begins at a young age, with private lessons and classes at school. Young musicians may attend music camps or festivals to polish their skills. Many use these opportunities to learn how to read music instead of just playing by ear.

It is not necessary to go to college to become a professional musician, but those performing classical music may get a bachelor's degree in music theory or performance. Bar-Josef studied at the Curtis Institute of Music in Philadelphia and the Julliard School in New York, and there are colleges across the United States that offer music programs. Being accepted into a college's music program often involves auditioning, submitting a recording, or both. Students in a bachelor's degree program learn about music theory, various music styles, and music history. They learn to improve their technique and expression. Business classes such as marketing can be helpful, since musicians are often self-employed and need to market themselves to find work. A musician may also obtain a master's degree in fine arts or music.

Skills and Personality

In addition to superior musical ability, professional musicians must be dedicated and disciplined. Mastering an instrument can be frustrating, and musicians must practice consistently and work through the challenges that come with learning to play. They must also be able to accept rejection and bounce back after failure if an audition or a job does not work out. Drummer Alana Velvis spent a year in California writing music and performing with an all-female group, but after the group's investor ran out of money and stopped paying, she found herself broke. She left California to live with relatives in Colorado and look for other jobs in music, but she still has fond memories of the experience. "This was the dream for me, playing music all the time and being creative," she recalls. "It's what we're all trying to do. It was an amazing opportunity while it lasted."[13]

Musicians are often part of a group and interact with audiences, agents, producers, and other performers, making communication and interpersonal skills important. Networking and making connections are often integral to finding work. "All of us have had gigs and opportunities that we've been put on because of our friends or someone we're connected to,"[14] notes musician and music producer Terence Fisher.

Promotional skills are also an asset because they help musicians get the word out about their abilities and showcase a performance or recording. To promote his business, Boliver makes YouTube videos, posts on social media, and maintains a website.

On the Job

Not Working Nine to Five

There is no one telling acoustic guitarist Maneli Jamal how much time to spend working on his music each day, but that does not mean he is not driven to play, record, edit, and mix. "I have so much music that I'm currently working on, so I'm constantly editing," he says. "I'm very motivated to get things done."[15] When first starting out, he played for up to eight hours a day. Now he generally teaches guitar between 11:00 a.m. and 2:00 p.m. and then plays music for an hour or two. He also spends several hours editing, mixing, and looking for new ideas for his music.

Musicians do not have typical nine-to-five work schedules. They may rehearse or perform during the day or night and could play gigs during the workweek or on the weekend. They might practice their music at home in the morning, head to a recording studio in the afternoon, and end up at a concert hall, stadium, or banquet facility in the evening to perform. Their audiences often differ depending on the venue. They could perform at special events such as weddings, quinceañeras, bar and bat mitzvah ceremonies, retirement celebrations, or other private events. At other times, they might play in front of a small crowd at a club, bar, church, or restaurant or in front of thousands of people at a music festival.

Some musicians perform alone. Others perform with a band, orchestra, or ensemble. In any case, the music they play can stir feelings, provide inspiration, and deliver enjoyment to listeners.

A concert tour can involve spending weeks on the road. When drummer Shawn Crowder is traveling with his band Sungazer as an opening act, the tour bus leaves for the next stop as soon as all the equipment is packed up after a show. He sleeps on the bus and the next morning unloads equipment at the new venue. In the afternoon the equipment is set up onstage and a sound check is done around five o'clock. He and his bandmates have some time to eat and hang out before the show, and after performing they head to the merchandise table to sell T-shirts and CDs. Then it is time to pack up the equipment, get on the bus, and head to the next stop. "All that work, every zip tie, cable, and label, the long hours in a cramped bus, the time away from home, so that we can do this for 45 minutes each evening,"[16] Crowder says.

A Satisfying Career

"I'm very happy with where I've been able to get in my career. I'm keeping it in line with music, and am not abandoning it for the random 9 to 5. I'm grateful that I'm still able to play music. I've relaxed on the idea of needing to be a performing, touring artist in order to feel successful as a musician. Any opportunity to play is great for me. Playing in my own venue, with my husband backing me up, is such a great experience."

—Alana Velvis, drummer and music café owner

Alana Velvis, interview by the author, October 16, 2024.

Self-Employment

Musicians are often self-employed, and many need to juggle multiple jobs to make ends meet. While working in Denver, Velvis was a drummer in a music program for babies and toddlers, taught private and group percussion lessons, and played in tribute bands. After marrying, she moved to New York and now works as an administrator for a company offering in-home music lessons. She and her husband also own a music café, where she sometimes performs. "As a musician you really need to be diverse," she says. "It's very hard to get paid to play the music you want to play only in the situations you want to play in. I want to play drums so I will play drums wherever people want to me to play drums."[17]

Caleb J. Murphy's goal is to be a full-time musician, but until that happens, he spends about half his workweek playing music and the rest writing blog posts for musicians, producing and mixing music for artists, editing podcasts, and posting content. "Most full-time musicians are blue-collar, middle-class musicians," Murphy notes. "They're making a living, yes. They can pay rent and their bills, and maybe they can afford fun stuff now and then. But they're not rich."[18]

Earnings and Employers

Musicians earn an average of $52,739 a year, according to 2025 statistics from the job website Indeed. The highest paid earn more than $86,000 annually, while the lowest paid earn about $32,000 a year. The average hourly salary for a musician is $35.69 per hour, according to Indeed.

Both Boliver and Fisher have worked as musical directors for a church, and the Bureau of Labor Statistics (BLS) notes that 30 percent of musicians and singers work for religious, civic, or professional organizations. Fifty-three percent are self-employed, according to the BLS, and 13 percent work in the performing arts. Three percent work in educational services.

What Is the Future Outlook for Musicians?

The careers website CareerExplorer expects employment of musicians to grow by 1.2 percent by 2032. This is slower than the growth rate of 4 percent that the BLS anticipates for all occupations. CareerExplorer anticipates about eight thousand job openings to occur for musicians by 2032. Most jobs will open up when existing musicians retire, but about twenty-one hundred additional jobs for musicians are expected to be created during that time period. The BLS notes that demand for live music will drive the need for musicians, although lower attendance at classical music performances and a decline in church participation could slow employment growth.

Find Out More

Berklee College of Music

https://college.berklee.edu

The website for the Berklee College of Music offers a good overview of an educational path for students interested in becoming a musician or studying other aspects of music. The “What Do You

Want to Study?" tool allows students to find information about undergraduate programs, summer and precollege programs, and other areas of study.

Juilliard School

www.juilliard.edu/music

This website for the prestigious Juilliard School offers insights into what it takes to become a professional musician. A video includes interviews with students and staff members, and information is available for those who play orchestral instruments, piano, organ, and guitar. Jazz studies are also featured.

NAMM Foundation

https://careers.namm.org

The website from an organization supporting music education provides information about a variety of careers in music. It explains various educational paths, including formal education, internships, apprenticeships, and private lessons.

What Does an Event Planner Do?

Angela Hatem has had unique experiences as an event planner. She had to help locate a missing child in a crowd of four hundred thousand. She has used PayPal to send an artist $10,000 right before a show so the artist would go onstage. She has also had her share of amazing experiences. "Only in a job like this would you get to sing karaoke with a two-hit-wonder pop band or spend $80,000 of someone else's money on fireworks,"[19] she notes.

Ruby Miles's goal is to attract people to the Laneway Festival in Australia and to help make sure the crowd has a great time. But when she is booking the event's musical acts, she knows she is taking a risk. "We sometimes book artists far in advance and hope their star rises at the right time so people will get excited and come to Laneway," she says. "It means there are moments where we think 'Oh god, will anyone want to come?'"[20]

At a Glance

Number of Jobs
132,000

Pay
$55,729

Educational Requirements
Bachelor's degree

Personal Qualities
Good communicator and negotiator, well organized, problem solver

Working Conditions
Office, on-site at concert or event venue

Future Job Outlook
Growth of 7.5 percent by 2032

Event planners in the music industry bring in artists and take care of countless details to ensure that everything at an event goes according to plan. They contact venues, hire musical acts, work out contracts, and set up the performance schedule, but they might also arrange for the artists' transportation, hotel rooms, and meals, as well as contract with the vendors who provide food and beverages at the event. Their duties could include securing the necessary permits from local governments and arranging for security, insurance, and the delivery of portable restrooms. They need to stay within the event's budget without sacrificing quality and must multitask when questions, concerns, challenges, and changes arise. A career as an event planner is more of a mission than a job, Hatem notes, since the event planner could be called on to do anything that is needed to make the event a success.

In addition to paying attention to the elements that make an event enjoyable, event planners need to be aware of what could go wrong. They must prepare for worst-case scenarios, including injuries, deaths, active shooters, crowd surges, and unruly fans. But more often they must anticipate milder crises, such as power outages, lighting or sound mishaps, and bad weather. For example, in June 2024 the singer Ludacris was onstage at an outdoor festival in southern Milwaukee County when storms moved in. Officials had to cancel the show and direct people to a safe location. "Our hope was that the storm, as it approached, would dissipate or move around similar to how it had throughout the day. That wasn't the case," says Joshua James, part of the event planning team. "So, once Ludacris went on stage we had to make that tough call of canceling the remainder of the event."[21]

How Do You Become an Event Planner?

Education and Training

An event planner usually has a bachelor's degree. The degree may be in event management, business, communications, or social science. Colleges also offer continuing education courses in event planning, allowing people already in the workforce to gain

Ready for Anything

"It's the kind of work in which there are truly no limits to the job-description bullet point: 'Other duties as assigned.' A client's request can happen out of the blue with zero time to spare and can vary from the everyday to the over the top. You've got to be prepared for it all."

—Angela Hatem, event planner

Angela Hatem, "I Was an Event Planner for 20 Years. Here Are Some of the Wildest Things I Witnessed on the Job," Business Insider, December 18, 2021. www.businessinsider.com.

skills for this career. Miles studied media in college and was working for a radio station when she was recommended for a job with the Laneway Festival.

Her first job was collecting streaming and radio play data for artists, looking for those growing in popularity. She also wrote music reviews and made music playlists for the programming team. "Then I started helping out with socials and, since my background is in presenting, I quickly started making informational videos in front of the camera and artist interviews backstage,"[22] she says. She initially worked for the festival part time but within four years was helping book the festival lineup.

Certification and Licensing

To demonstrate knowledge and professional expertise, an event planner may obtain a certification. The Certified Meeting Professional credential is available from the Events Industry Council. Candidates for the certification must show proof of experience and education. Those who meet the requirements must pass an exam covering strategic planning, financial and risk management, logistics, and facility operations.

Booking Acts Is Not an Easy Job

"I think a lot of the time people look at lineups and think that we set out to get these 30 acts and booked them . . . in reality, we have a long wishlist of artists and we deal with a lot of rejection in the booking process. To those people always commenting 'Why didn't Laneway book ___?,' we most likely tried."

—Ruby Miles, programming and social media assistant for the Laneway Festival

Quoted in Izzy Wight, "How I Got Here: Laneway's Assistant Programmer on Why You Should Use Social Media as Your Resume," *Fashion Journal*, January 18, 2024. https://fashionjournal.com.au.

Volunteer Work and Internships

To gain experience in event planning, students can plan events at their college or university. They can also shadow professionals and volunteer or work at a local festival or event to connect with those in the industry. Miles notes that to get a job at a music festival, newcomers should be enthusiastic about the event or music in general. "The best thing to convey to the employer is that you're a fan—you live and breathe live music or music on TikTok or music journalism," she says. "If you're passionate about it, you won't necessarily need skills to get started." She adds that networking is important. "This industry goes by word of mouth a lot of the time. I recommend using your social media almost like a resume. Post the festivals you volunteer at or start a music review TikTok account—anything to show your interest!"[23]

Skills and Personality

Communication and interpersonal skills are assets for event planners. They use oral and written communication to hire personnel, bring in acts, and secure service contractors. They need to communicate clearly to make sure others understand what is expected of them and to maintain positive relationships with the people they work with. Negotiation skills are also important, since event planners work within a budget that accounts for performer, security, and staff pay as well as costs related to the venue, licensing, equipment, and every other detail that will make an event successful.

On the Job

Working Conditions

Event planners usually work in an office while an event is being planned, but in the days leading up to a concert, festival, or other event, they often spend time in the venue or on the festival grounds. Although they usually work full time, they will often put in additional hours shortly before and during an event. Working on Saturday and Sunday is part of the job when an event takes place over the weekend. They get to relax a bit after the festival is over, but then they must soon begin planning for the next event.

Event planners juggle many details and therefore must be organized and adept at multitasking. They also need to anticipate problems and have a plan for resolving them. The festival Joshua James works with has a weather center where event teams gather with local police and fire officials to discuss how to handle incoming storms. That helped him and his team devise a plan to ensure that the Ludacris fans were directed to safety when the storms rolled in.

If unexpected problems arise, event coordinators need to react quickly and calmly. Matt Laughlin's career has taken him from event planning to event facility director, and he has been the one people turn to when an issue needs to be resolved. This can involve everything from venue parking to crowd management. "Two tour buses and two semi-trucks show up for the big show, loaded, and you'd have to reroute them down one-way streets and obtain city permits to park and unload," he explains. "If patrons are showing up with only 15 minutes to spare and there's a line out the door, it would come down to how do we get 2,000 people in and seated in the next 10 minutes."[24]

An experienced event planner may become an operations coordinator or festival director. Gaining experience in the field helps an individual understand the many facets of running an event, from traffic flow to food and beverage coordination to where the portable bathrooms should be placed. In some cases an event encompasses more than music, and the coordinator needs to oversee multiple spaces and activities. The Ashley for the Arts event in Eau Claire, Wisconsin, for example, features arts and crafts booths, a lumberjack show, hot air balloons, and events for children, in addition to musical acts. "I'm not sure that everybody recognizes that it's more than just a music festival," says Bailey Waldera, event manager. "There is just so much."[25]

Earnings

Event planners have an average yearly salary of $55,729, according to 2025 information from the jobs website Indeed. The highest paid make more than $89,000 a year, while the lowest paid make around $35,000. The average hourly pay for event planners is $23.24 per hour. Over the past ten years, the pay for event planners has gone up by about 9 percent.

What Is the Future Outlook for Event Planners?

The future for event planners looks good; the website CareerExplorer expects employment of event planners to grow by 7.5 percent through 2032. This is faster than the average for all occupations. CareerExplorer anticipates 16,200 job openings by 2032. It estimates that 9,900 additional event planners will be needed and 6,300 people will need to fill roles currently held by people who are retiring.

For Laughlin, the hard work of planning an event is worth it when he sees an audience seated for a performance. "We'd see an auditorium full of patrons, whether it's a symphony show, a National Geographic lecture, or the Ellen DeGeneres Netflix special," he says. "A lot of people are involved to make it happen. That's really rewarding."[26]

Find Out More

AEG Worldwide

www.aegworldwide.com/careers

Through AEG Presents, AEG Worldwide puts on festivals around the world, including the Coachella Valley Music and Arts Festival in California and the New Orleans Jazz & Heritage Festival. Its careers website features videos from people who work in different areas of the company, including event management and festival marketing.

International Festivals & Events Association (IFEA)

www.ifea.com

The IFEA supports professionals in this field. Its website includes information about scholarships for training and attendance at the organization's annual convention. The IFEA also offers webinars and a weeklong event management school geared toward new and mid-career industry professionals.

Live Nation

www.livenation.com

Live Nation presents large music festivals and concerts as well as smaller club shows. Its website provides information about what it is like to work at Live Nation as well as the benefits offered to employees.

What Does a DJ Do?

When DJ Will Gill is working, he is doing a lot of thinking, planning, and reacting when deciding which songs to play. "A good DJ is someone who entertains, chooses music, sets trends, and most importantly, knows how to control the mood of a crowd,"[27] Gill explains.

Though the abbreviation once referred primarily to radio DJs (or disc jockeys), event DJs perform for audiences at clubs, weddings, corporate functions, music festivals, and concerts. They set the tone by blending songs and beats, often enhancing their stage show with lights and even fireworks. By tapping into the crowd's urge to dance, they control an event's atmosphere, skillfully keeping the crowd engaged in a dynamic and lively experience. They might excite a crowd with a set of familiar and well-loved tracks or use software and tools to blend pieces of music with sounds of guitars, organs, and drums as they create electronic dance music in the moment.

A reputation for delivering a good time can make a DJ the main attraction at an event or club. Martin Garrix of the Netherlands, who

At a Glance

Number of Jobs
21,000

Pay
$20 per hour

Educational Requirements
High school diploma

Personal Qualities
Good communicator, business skills, tech-savvy, interpersonal skills, persistence

Working Conditions
Events, festivals

Future Job Outlook
5 percent growth through 2033

is consistently ranked as one of the world's top DJs, draws huge crowds in Las Vegas, Colombia, Spain, Chile, and Greece. He also spends time in the studio producing danceable music for clubs and festivals as well as pop songs, like his 2013 breakout hit "Animals."

A mobile DJ may operate on a smaller scale, providing musical entertainment at local events. That is how Garrix got his start as a teen. "I would have a portable DJ setup, so I would play weddings and school parties,"[28] he recalls. Other types of DJs include scratch DJs and turntablists, who use vinyl records and scratching techniques in performances and competitions. A DJ could also work behind the scenes at a business event or lounge with a low-key vibe, using music selections to establish a quiet, relaxed, or professional atmosphere.

How Do You Become a DJ?

Training

DJs must have a deep knowledge of music, including artists, songs, lyrics, genres, and trends, so they can create the right sound for the right moment. They need to understand how to mix songs and blend beats, harmonies, and tempos to generate a set or sound that matches the energy of an event.

It is also necessary for DJs to be skilled at using electronic music equipment. DJs may have a high school diploma or college degree in music, audio production, or another field. They need to have the technical skills required to use the software and equipment that allows them to put together set lists, develop electronic dance music, and present their product to a crowd. A sound production company may provide on-the job training, or DJs can learn basic techniques through online videos and tutorials or in-person classes. That instruction will help them master the controllers and software to manage beat grids, export playlists, create a mix, and perform a set. They can also learn more advanced

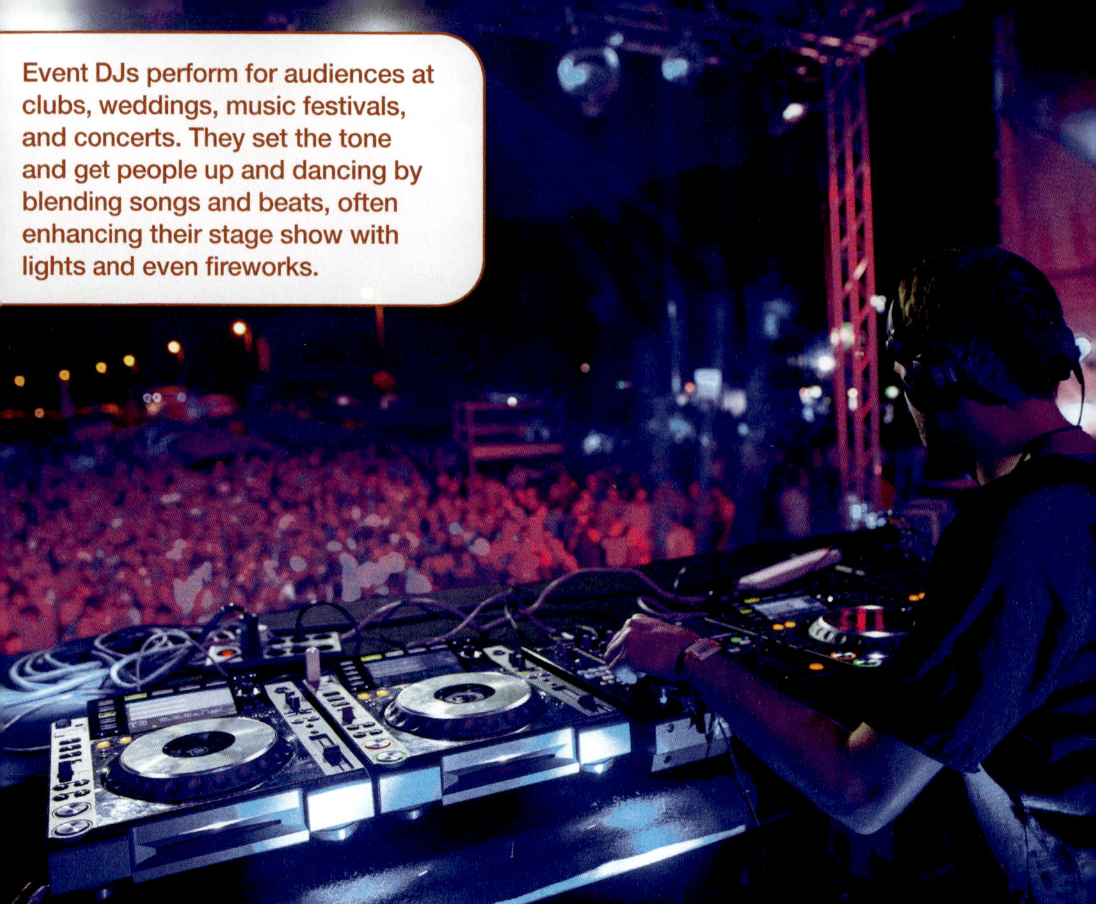

Event DJs perform for audiences at clubs, weddings, music festivals, and concerts. They set the tone and get people up and dancing by blending songs and beats, often enhancing their stage show with lights and even fireworks.

techniques in harmonic and a cappella mixing, scratching, filters, loops, audio effects, and tempo adjustments. To produce their own electronic dance music, they need an understanding of how to compile and edit mixes to build tracks and create their signature sound. DJs often create custom audio clips called DJ drops that they use to introduce themselves to an audience or producer as they switch from one track to another.

Skills and Personality

A passion for music often drives a DJ to gain these skills. Tyler Morris, who DJs as Westend, became obsessed with music as a teen after seeing a performance by French DJ Gesaffelstein (Mike Lévy). "I was like, this is gonna be my personality," he says. Seeing a friend DJ at an event also inspired his career. "I want to be the one behind the decks kind of controlling energy, the room,"[29] he says. He bought his own controller and learned about electronic music production in a digital music lab at the Bronx High School of Science in New York. He continued to pursue music and play gigs while studying public policy at Duke University. He cofounded a website that offers instruction for aspiring DJs and continues to play gigs and produce songs. "I want to be able to make music that you want to listen to on a road trip, and that you want to listen to in a club,"[30] he says.

DJs need to stay on top of music trends, be perceptive about a crowd's reaction, and tailor their performance accordingly. When Garrix performs, he is aware of the mood of the dancers and the atmosphere of the venue, and those affect the music he chooses. "Every week there is a different crowd, a different vibe,"[31] he says.

Successful DJs need good communication and public speaking skills because they interact with crowds and talk with event managers, promoters, and others in the music business. Interpersonal skills are also important, since DJs negotiate with clients and may collaborate with other artists, as Garrix has done with DubVision and Shaun Farrugia to create tracks such as "Wherever You Are."

DJs are often self-employed, so they must have solid business skills to find and bill clients, budget for expenses, take care of taxes, and deal with other financial matters. Because marketing is often done through social media, DJs need to be comfortable creating and posting content to build a fan base. It can be difficult to gain a foothold as a professional DJ, and persistence is required to attract clients and maintain a steady source of income.

On the Job

Working Conditions

DJs typically perform at night and on weekends, but their work begins long before an event's start time. Weeks or months before the event, a DJ meets with the client to discuss the event's atmosphere and go over specific song requests and then crafts a playlist that matches the client's expectations. Travel arrangements are made, and a DJ may need to transport gear that could include mixers, turntables, microphones, and speakers.

Once on-site, it is often up to the DJ to set up and test the sound system. An event might be held indoors at a conference center, nightclub, or banquet hall or outside in an arena, on the grounds of a music festival, or on the beach. When Garrix plays at a beach hotel in Spain, for example, he needs to carefully monitor the weather. "If the humidity is higher, if the wind is coming towards me, it [affects] the sound," he explains. "There are so many things in play that make every week completely different."[32]

At an Event

During the event, DJs stand behind a turntable deck or controller. They might be onstage as the center of attention or off to the side of the room. When working at a wedding or corporate event, they often act as master of ceremonies and make announcements to keep the event on track. They also need to make sure everyone is having a good time. "It's about creating an atmosphere, setting the mood, and then taking the audience on a journey," Gill explains. "A good DJ needs to watch the crowd and change their music based on how people are reacting."[33] After the event ends, DJs pack up their equipment and travel home.

Taking Care of Business

During the day, DJs often take care of the business side of their job. DJ Shinski's day includes phone calls to clients, promoters, and other DJs. "Customer service, that's what takes a lot of my time," he says. "It's not all glamour." He may also talk with manag-

Energy and Encouragement

"I love feeling the adrenaline of shows, travel, tours, and the studio; this madness fuels my creativity and makes me produce more. Sometimes when I'm far from home I get a video call from my kids, and when I hear their voices everything changes: the fatigue fades, the longing lessens, and it cures any headache. My family is my daily dose of encouragement."

—Alok, Brazilian DJ

Quoted in DJ Mag, "Top 100 DJs 2024: 4 Alok." https://djmag.com.

ers who are assisting him in arranging a tour to Uganda, Tanzania, Kenya, and other African countries. They will help him arrange contracts, invoices, and logistics such as transportation. "I can't do all that on my own,"[34] says Shinski, who has more than 1 million YouTube subscribers. His day also may include streaming live on YouTube, creating social media content for sponsors, and working in the studio with a music producer. After he wraps up in the studio around 9:00 p.m., Shinski may head to a club for an evening performance.

Employers and Earnings

DJs make money from gigs, music downloads, and sponsorships. The median hourly wage for DJs was twenty dollars per hour in May 2023, according to the website CareerOneStop, which is sponsored by the US Department of Labor. This means half of DJs earned more than this amount and half earned less. The median wage of DJs is below the median hourly wage for all occupations of $23.11 per hour, although the highest-paid 10 percent of DJs earned more than $57.66 per hour. The lowest-paid 10 percent earned less than $11.08 per hour.

Focus on the Job, Not Negativity

"In the infancy of my career, a lot of doors were closed [because of my gender]. But I eventually stopped caring about negative opinions and will never let it affect me or my decision-making."

—Peggy Gou, DJ and music artist

Quoted in Margaux Anbouba, "Inside DJ Peggy Gou's Very Bold World," *Vogue*, May 29, 2024. www.vogue.com.

What Is the Future Outlook for DJs?

CareerOneStop reports that there were 21,000 people employed as DJs outside of radio in 2023, and this number is expected to grow by 5 percent to 22,100 through 2033. This is above the expected growth of 4 percent for all occupations. The states with the largest number of DJs are California, New York, Washington, Arizona, and Texas.

The growth has much to do with the demand for in-person performances and the broadening of what was once a male-dominated profession to include women and nonbinary DJs playing for more diverse audiences. Regardless, DJs will always be needed to entertain guests at weddings, parties, and corporate events and to create new electronic dance music that is presented at clubs and concerts.

Find Out More

DJ Mag

https://djmag.com

This London-based website provides news and features on DJs from around the world. Many of its articles focus on electronic dance music, and the tech section discusses new equipment and software. Videos feature artists talking about how they created their songs.

Kick & Bass

www.kick-bass.com

Tutorials on music production, coaching, and a DJ community for beginners can be found on this subscription-based website. DJs can also submit tracks, receive feedback, and watch weekly live streams from professional DJs.

Pioneer DJ

https://blog.pioneerdj.com

Tips for DJs and information about DJ culture are featured on the blog of DJ equipment maker Pioneer. Articles explain how to choose a DJ name, navigate a sleep schedule, and manage mental health. The history section offers a look at how technology has changed over the years.

What Does a Sound Engineer Do?

Sound engineer Nathan Bond has always been drawn to the technical side of music. "When I was a teenager, I had a little sound system in my basement, and I played in a band with my cousin," he recalls. Now a live sound engineer, he travels with a band and operates the console sending sound to the performers. "Everything that I do is what the artist hears, not the crowd," he explains. "Whatever they need to hear is what I do."[35]

In-studio sound engineer Isabel Gracefield finds that the best recording sessions have artists who know what they want and an engineer and others working toward that goal. "How that vision gets realized can take any form," says Gracefield, whose engineering clients have included pop star Dua Lipa. "I do think the core of the role is to be a cheerleader: to be the person in the room who is most in love with the music and keep[s] everyone on track and productive."[36]

Sound engineers record, mix, and reproduce music and vocals. Also called audio engineers, their work allows an audience to hear the best version of the sound created by a performer, musician, or

At a Glance

Number of Jobs
18,000

Pay
$59,430

Educational Requirements
Associate's or bachelor's degree

Personal Qualities
Communication skills, good hand-eye coordination, tech-savvy, problem-solving skills

Working Conditions
Recording studio or on location

Future Job Outlook
Decline of 1 percent through 2033

speaker. At a concert, live event, or recording session, it is their responsibility to ensure that the sound quality is up to the artist's standards. During a seminar or other event, an audience can clearly hear what is being said because of the sound engineer's expertise. A video game dialogue editor might clean up an audio recording to get rid of pops and clicks or make a voice sound like an alien. Sound engineers also create the sounds that make a video game realistic, synchronize sound effects in a movie, allow playgoers to hear the actors' dialogue, and make sure a podcast sounds polished.

How Do You Become a Sound Engineer?

Education and Training

Sound engineers may have an associate's or bachelor's degree in audio engineering or a related field, such as communications technology or music. Audio engineering courses are also available through nondegree certificate programs, and YouTube videos offer instruction in how to use sound mixing equipment and software.

Volunteering and Internships

Helpful high school classes for sound engineers include math, physics, and electronics. Sound engineers need training to run the equipment, software, and other technology used to record, edit, and mix sounds. Practice working with this equipment is essential. While educational programs offer hands-on instruction, audio engineering students can also gain experience by running the sound for school productions and community theater groups. A dialogue editor might work on student-related games and films. Sound engineering students may also have an internship with a recording studio or game company start-up.

Skills and Personality

Physical work is often involved in a sound engineer's job. At a live performance, sound engineers may set up and take down microphones, amplifiers, speakers, a mixing board, and other equipment. They also repair and take care of sound equipment.

A sound engineer looking to work in a recording studio should be a music fan and enjoy working with audio equipment and software. A fascination with audio technology drew in Sierra Noble, an audio engineer, artist, and producer. "I've always been in awe of all the gear in the studios,"[37] she says.

When equipment does not work as expected, audio engineers use problem-solving skills, patience, and persistence to resolve the issue. As a monitor engineer, one of Kelly Kramarik's worst enemies is the screeching sound of feedback that develops when the speaker picks up the frequency from the microphone. When the pitch starts to ring out, she must immediately identify the frequency and make the right adjustments to get it to stop as soon as possible.

Sound engineers also need good people skills. When working with performers or recording artists, sound engineers need to set their ego and personal musical tastes aside and strive to achieve what the artist is looking for. "You are not the star," notes Justin Colletti, a mastering engineer who has taught audio engineering courses. "You do not decide exactly how things should sound. You're a facilitator; you're providing services to someone else."[38]

Sound engineers must have good hand-eye coordination for adjusting the knobs, dials, and sliders on a console. They should also enjoy learning, since recording technology is ever-changing. A professional sound engineer may attend continuing education courses or receive on-the-job training to stay on top of the latest technological advances.

Certification

To let employers know that they meet industry standards, sound engineers may become certified. The Society of Broadcast Engi-

Experiment to Find a Signature Sound

"Sometimes I amuse myself by putting completely the wrong microphone in the wrong place, and smashing it through a Distressor, just to see what happens. It's great when you have that level of trust in a setup to be able to play around. Seeing such a range come out of each room has helped me develop my own signature."

—Isabel Gracefield, audio engineer

Quoted in William Stokes, "Talkback: Isabel Gracefield," *Sound on Sound*, May 2021. www.soundonsound.com.

neers offers certification and continuing education opportunities. A sound engineer can become a Certified Technology Specialist through the Audiovisual and Integrated Experience Association by meeting eligibility requirements and passing an exam.

On the Job

In the Studio

Gracefield, who has spent much of her career at RAK Studios in London, began working as an assistant to in-house engineers. The job gave her the opportunity to ask questions and see how the recording team worked together. "Beyond picking up a language of mic and gear choices, I also got to see different styles of interpersonal relationships between the engineer and the producer and the artist,"[39] she recalls.

A recording session typically starts at 10:00 a.m. and can last twelve hours or more. Before beginning a project, Gracefield listens to reference tracks suggested by the producer or artist to gain an understanding of the sound they are looking for. "I do a huge amount of planning and prep with colorcoded spreadsheets," she explains. "Pre-session me does all the boring stuff

Sound engineers record, mix, and reproduce music and vocals. Whether at a concert, live event, or recording session, their job is to make sure the audience hears the best version of the performer's work.

so that on-session me doesn't need to, and that opens up the headspace for looking after the producer and artist's needs."[40]

At a Live Performance

When working as a monitor engineer during a live performance at a music festival, there is little time between acts to prepare, so Kramarik is constantly alert to what the band wants from her. "Maybe while they're walking onstage they say, 'I want kick, snare, and bass in my mix' and I say, 'Okay,' and then I just kind of pull it up a little bit," she says. Band members use hand signals to let her know what they need to hear, and they depend on her to get it right. "You want to make their performance go off without a hitch," she says. "If they can't hear everything, that's just not gonna happen."[41]

Varied Working Conditions and Hours

Sound engineers may work inside at a recording studio, conference center, or performance venue or outdoors at a concert or music festival. They work into the night or on weekends when they need to meet a deadline or when on tour with a performer. Nathan Bond notes that touring can be tiring and tough on his family, and setting up equipment at a venue can be challenging, but the job itself is enjoyable.

Employers and Earnings

Sound engineers often freelance or work independently rather than for a single company, and networking is vital to building a career. Kramarik has advanced her career by meeting people and asking questions. "I ask them how their studio works, who they hire, how all of that goes, and if they have any opportunities," she says. "I'm always looking for new opportunities, and if someone ever brings one my way, I say, 'Yes.'"[42]

Most sound engineers work in motion picture and video industries and sound recording industries, according to the Bureau of Labor Statistics. Other industries employing sound technicians include event promoters and radio and television broadcasting stations. Sound engineers may also work for colleges, universities, and professional schools. Recording industry hubs in the United States are where many sound engineers find employment. Therefore, California, New York, Florida, Maryland, and Tennessee have the highest number of jobs for sound engineers. The median salary for sound engineers was $59,430 in 2023. This means half earned above this amount, and half earned below it.

A sound technician may begin working for a smaller company or market and move to a larger one after obtaining experience and additional skills. A video game sound designer, for example, can get a start by working on smaller projects with independent companies or gaming communities and then make more lucrative connections by attending the Game Developers Conference, which is held annually.

Connect with Others in the Business

"Try to learn as much as you can and talk to other people because you might learn a lot just by being like, 'Hey what's your studio?' If you're like, hey I want to come help, there's always room in audio for that kind of thing."

—J Riley Hill, freelance audio engineer

Quoted in What Do You Do?, "Why Being an Audio Engineer Is So Cool," YouTube, February 1, 2023. www.youtube.com/watch?v=uOEltzAF5L8.

What Is the Future Outlook for Sound Engineers?

There were 18,000 sound engineering jobs in 2023, according to the Bureau of Labor Statistics. The number of sound engineering jobs is expected to drop to 17,900 by 2033. Sound engineers will still be needed to create quality sound effects for movies, shows, and video games and to record voices, music, and sounds. Advances in technology mean that fewer sound engineers will be needed to set up and operate sound systems, however, and that in part explains the anticipated decline.

However, the human touch is still important in this career; having an ear for the right chords or the effectiveness of ambient sounds is crucial to hit songs and movie or game soundtracks alike. Those with a passion for the job who are willing to put in the time can build a good career, notes freelance audio engineer J Riley Hill. "The money is okay," he says, "and the job itself is really fun."[43]

Find Out More

Audio Engineering Society

https://aes2.org

The Audio Engineering Society is an international organization devoted to audio technology. Its website includes industry news and offers information about conferences, conventions, and training.

Audiovisual and Integrated Experience Association (AVIXA)
www.avixa.org
The website for AVIXA offers a look at standards, training, and certifications for audiovisual professionals. Articles offer technical information, and its training programs include a general knowledge course that provides foundational training for audiovisual design, installation, and management. It also offers courses relating to technology used at live events.

Society of Broadcast Engineers
https://sbe.org
The website for the association supporting broadcast and multimedia technology professionals offers information about broadcast engineering jobs and careers. It provides webinars on technical topics and information about certification exams in several areas. High school and college students studying broadcast engineering or a related field can join the organization.

Sound on Sound
www.soundonsound.com
News about audio technology and reviews of the latest equipment are featured on the website of *Sound on Sound* magazine. The website's *SOS Podcasts* feature interviews with people working in music production. In the "People" section, engineers, recording artists, and others in the recording industry offer insights on topics relating to sound production.

What Do Agents and Managers Do?

As a manager for music artists, Imowo Udo-Utun, known as Veli, makes dreams come true. "Helping an artist grow, tour the world, achieve their dreams and provide for their family is success for me,"[44] he says.

Agent Stefanie Purificati makes connections that give her clients an opportunity to perform. She often travels to check out music clubs and does not hesitate to call venue operators, festival managers, and others who might be interested in booking the music artists she represents. "The job of an agent is at its core a sales job," she explains. "I act as a liaison between the buyer and my artist and I'm always trying to negotiate the best deal possible for my client."[45]

Agents and managers guide the careers of performing artists, handling the business side of things so the artist can concentrate on showcasing musical or vocal skills without being concerned about bookings or contract details. An agent is often an artist's touring expert, making connections that lead to bands and singers being booked for shows and tours. The agent may repre-

At a Glance

Number of Jobs
18,600

Pay
$84,900

Educational Requirements
Bachelor's degree

Personal Qualities
Communication and negotiation skills, active listener, good at problem solving and critical thinking

Working Conditions
Office, travel to concerts and events

Future Job Outlook
Growth of 9 percent through 2033

sent the artist during contract negotiations and work out travel logistics. Managers set a strategy for a client's career, establish a marketing plan, and contact people who can help the artist's music reach an audience. To make sure his artists are heard, Veli has a goal of making at least one contact every day. In addition, managers and agents handle a multitude of details and are there to support artists when things do not work out and celebrate with them when they do.

How Do You Become an Agent or Manager?

Education, Training, and Connections

Agents usually have a four-year bachelor's degree, and some have a master's degree. It is vital to gain experience working with artists and music management. Veli was a business major when he began managing his friend's rap music career while in college. When he discovered that there were not many performing opportunities in his area, he began organizing concerts. After college he became a manager with the music management service Sounds Music Group.

Justin LaMotte was a marketing major in college and began organizing concerts to pay for school. Some artists from the concerts asked him to help them manage their careers, and after graduation he interned for a music management company to learn more about the inner workings of a larger organization. He left to manage an artist, and he and a partner founded the management company Black Wax to work with new talent. "I just kind of fell in love with the idea of working with artists and being able to find opportunities for them and help shed light on their talent,"[46] he says.

Internships

An internship also helped manager Basak Kizilisik gain a foothold in the music industry. She tried majoring in premed and prelaw in college but found that neither was her passion. She wanted a career that allowed her to connect musicians and fans, and she got an internship with a music video director for whom she did everything from taking out the trash and working at the front desk to editing concept documents for videos. She was also a production assistant for music video shoots. "I got great experience on the creative side, like how to bring a story to life, how to tell a story with a visual medium, and how that can play a major role on the music side of things," she says. She moved on to jobs in publishing and digital marketing and worked for a music label and in marketing for an artist management firm—all before establishing her own management company. "I just knew that I wanted to learn as much as I could about the business before I asked an artist to put their career in my hands," Kizilisik says. "I got a little taste of all of it and I'm really glad. It makes me a lot more of an effective manager now."[47]

Skills and Personality

Agents and managers must have good communication, interpersonal, and speaking skills, since they need to establish a relationship with their client and then work with others to promote the client's talents. Meetings must be scheduled with the right people to bring needed exposure for their clients. They negotiate with promoters, unions, and others, influencing people to look at things from their point of view without damaging the relationship. Because meetings must go well so work can be secured for clients, active listening is an important skill for agents and managers. This involves paying attention to other speakers, asking questions, and carefully considering the points being made without interrupting. Complaints must be handled diplomatically, and disputes and conflicts need to be settled. Good judgment and critical-thinking skills are important, since agents and managers anticipate problems that can occur, evaluate options, and make choices that impact an artist's career.

Knowledge of business and accounting are also needed because agents collect fees, commissions, and other payments for clients. They are also involved in contract negotiations and must

To Learn About Managing, Study Managers

"Find artist managers and execs that you look up to. Study them, look at their podcast interviews, and study what they did and their journey. You can also look at different artists that you look up to or admire and look up their managers and study them. You have to be a sponge, you have to soak up the information, you have to be willing to be that fly on the wall and study, observe and take the good and bad that you see and mold your own morals values and how you want to shape your own company."

—Imowo Udo-Utun, known as Veli, music artist manager

Quoted in Music Forward Foundation, *Day in the Life: Artist Management—Industry Sessions*, YouTube, February 29, 2024. www.youtube.com/watch?v=Q62VG_VN3Wg.

understand the details involved. Organizational skills are used to juggle the many tasks required to set up gigs and tours. For example, they must coordinate venues, hotels, meals, and other logistics for a touring performer. As an artist's career grows and additional staff members are brought on to handle specific duties, managers delegate and use administration skills to determine where money and time are best spent.

Agents and managers need to stay on top of marketing and social media trends so they can effectively promote their clients via websites, social media, and interviews. They need to keep up with changes in music culture as well. Managers and agents shoulder the responsibility for their artists' careers and are often under pressure to deliver results. Handling the criticism that can come with this requires a thick skin. "You are going to be the blame for every loss and you're going to not get the congratulations for every success or win, and you have to be okay with that,"[48] LaMotte notes.

On the Job

In the Office

Purificati spends much of her day on the phone, talking with people who may have an interest in her clients. Agents and managers need to be comfortable calling strangers, she notes, and a phone call allows her to convey her passion for the artist in a way that an email cannot. The music business is built on relationships, and getting her message to the right people is an important part of her job.

Tour stops and festival appearances may need to be planned more than a year in advance, and Purificati connects with clients to discuss these plans. An agent or manager's day may also involve a meeting with the artist's label, arranging a radio or podcast interview, handling emails, assessing songs, working on a social media post, considering the next steps in the artist's career, and making sure the artist gets enough rest before a performance.

On the Road

At night and on the weekend, agents and managers may attend networking events, go to shows, and field calls. They need a good knowledge of the venues where their artists perform, so on the weekends Purificati often travels to clubs or festivals. This provides her with information she can share with her clients, and she notes that club managers are more likely to take her calls if she has been there in person.

When on the road with clients, Veli handles tour management duties. He makes sure the schedule is set, technical and production details are in place, food has been ordered, and finances are taken care of. He also takes care of any issues that emerge. "You gotta be like an octopus," he says. "You may wake up doing one thing, but there might be eight other things to handle instead."[49]

Earnings

Agents and managers do not typically earn salaries but instead are paid a commission—a percentage of the money earned by their

Checking Out Venues Is Part of the Job

"Some artists can't play in different kinds of venues like churches or different rooms with different kinds of sounds, and I need to know what kind of venue they're going into so that I can plan my tours accordingly. The same thing applies for festivals as well. I need to know what kind of audience is at a festival, so I go to a lot of festivals during the summer and get to know the people who are running the festivals, get to know the people who are attending."

—Stefanie Purificati, booking agent

Quoted in MusiCounts, *Track: Career Profiles—a Day in the Life of a Booking Agent with Stefanie Purificati*, YouTube, June 3, 2021. www.youtube.com/watch?v=jaUFBptd1RY.

clients. They may receive 10 percent of the booking fee earned by the artist, for example, or 15 to 20 percent of an artist's income.

Experienced agents typically earn wages that are above the national average. Agents had a median wage of $40.82 per hour in 2023, according to the Bureau of Labor Statistics, and a median annual wage of $84,900. This means that half of the agents earned more than this amount and half earned less. These wages are above the median wage for all occupations of $23.11 per hour, or $48,060 per year. Income grows as an agent gains experience. CareerExplorer notes that music management graduates typically earn a salary of $42,909 early in their career. Those with five years of experience earn $51,430, and those with ten years of experience earn around $61,000.

What Is the Future Outlook for Agents and Managers?

The future outlook for agents is bright. CareerOneStop projects job growth of 9 percent through 2033, which is much faster than average. There were 18,600 people employed as agents in 2023, and there are 2,100 projected openings through 2033. Most jobs for agents and business managers or artists and performers are in California, New York, Tennessee, Florida, and North Carolina, where recording industries are prevalent.

Find Out More

International Entertainment Buyers Association

www.ieba.org

The International Entertainment Buyers Association is a nonprofit trade organization for industry professionals. The "Educational Outreach" tab on its website offers information about scholarships. The website also offers networking opportunities for members, including membership mixers and a conference.

International Radio and Television Society Foundation

https://irtsfoundation.org

The goal of the International Radio and Television Society Foundation is to build leaders and increase diversity in the media industry. It offers academic programs, industry events, and mentorship opportunities. Information about the organization's summer fellowship program can also be found on the website.

United Talent Agency

www.unitedtalent.com

The website for the United Talent Agency artist management firm has information about music artists and others represented by its company. A "Careers" section offers information about internships and the company's agent training program for young professionals. Its "News and Stories" section features interviews with agents who represent artists in a variety of fields.

Source Notes

Introduction: Pursuing a Creative Career in Music

1. Jillissa Anderson, "Music Career Options: Sharing Alternatives for Young Musicians," School Band and Orchestra, August 8, 2024. https://sbomagazine.com.
2. Quoted in Jamie, "Louise Lelièvre," HowWeListen, April 25, 2024. https://byta.com.
3. Quoted in Artina McCain, "Building Diversity in Your Music Career," *Piano Magazine*, Winter 2020–2021, p. 45.
4. Alana Velvis, interview by the author, October 16, 2024.

Music Therapist

5. Jane Creagan, "Career Options," American Music Therapy Association. https://musictherapy-assets-new.azureedge.net.
6. Quoted in CreativeVibesMT, *The Difference Between a Music Therapist, Teacher, and Musician: Music Therapy Advocacy and Education*, YouTube, January 5, 2023. www.youtube.com/watch?v=DMgVEq7BxGU.
7. Quoted in CreativeVibesMT, *The Difference Between a Music Therapist, Teacher, and Musician*.
8. Quoted in Kristine Thompson, "A Day in the Life of Two Music Therapists," University of Rochester, 2021. www.rochester.edu.
9. Quoted in CreativeVibesMT, *3 Downsides of Being a Music Therapist—Realities of a Music Therapy Career*, YouTube, November 3, 2022. www.youtube.com/watch?v=ADm0jQLOqYg.
10. Quoted in Thompson, "A Day in the Life of Two Music Therapists."

Musician

11. Quoted in Full Circle Music, *How I Became a Full-Time Musician and You Can Too*, YouTube, January 24, 2022. www.youtube.com/watch?v=X2MrIJC2fHg.
12. Quoted in WETA Classical, "What Is a Concertmaster in an Orchestra? Nurit Bar-Josef of the NSO Explains," *Classical Breakdown*, YouTube, July 18, 2023. www.youtube.com/watch?v=MHtqKtiuD3s.
13. Velvis, interview.

14. Terence Fisher, *How to Build a Sustainable Music Career (Tips for Musicians)*, YouTube, September 2, 2024. www.youtube.com/watch?v=3SO2q--Trng.
15. Maneli Jamal, *My Daily Routine as a Musician*, YouTube, October 21, 2021. www.youtube.com/watch?v=1oFyk1l_pFk.
16. Shawn Crowder, *Day in the Life of a Touring Musician*, YouTube, July 20, 2023. www.youtube.com/watch?v=pSxxZ5XAB8o.
17. Velvis, interview.
18. Caleb J. Murphy, "Being a Full-Time Musician Is Not for the Weak," *Digital Music News*, November 17, 2023. www.digitalmusicnews.com.

Event Planner

19. Angela Hatem, "I Was an Event Planner for 20 Years. Here Are Some of the Wildest Things I Witnessed on the Job," Business Insider, December 18, 2021. www.businessinsider.com.
20. Quoted in Izzy Wight, "How I Got Here: Laneway's Assistant Programmer on Why You Should Use Social Media as Your Resume," *Fashion Journal*, January 18, 2024. https://fashionjournal.com.au.
21. Quoted in Ryan Jenkins, "Festival Organizer Details Emergency Planning After Severe Weather Forces Show to End Early," TMJ4, June 24, 2024. www.tmj4.com.
22. Quoted in Wight, "How I Got Here."
23. Quoted in Wight, "How I Got Here."
24. Quoted in Carol Marino, "On with the Show—FVCC Taps Seattle Pro for the New College Center's Director," *Kalispell (MT) Daily Inter Lake*, January 17, 2022. https://dailyinterlake.com.
25. Quoted in Regev Nystrom, "Ashley for the Arts Marks 15 Years of Showcasing Music," *Eau Claire (WI) Leader-Telegram*, August 2, 2024. www.leadertelegram.com.
26. Quoted in Marino, "On with the Show."

DJ

27. DJ Will Gill, "What Is the Most Important Job of a DJ?," DJ Will Gill personal website, February 23, 2024. https://djwillgill.com.
28. Quoted in DJ Mag, "Top 100 DJs 2024: 1 Martin Garrix." https://djmag.com.
29. Quoted in Gray Area, "Westend: Artist Spotlight," 2025. https://grayarea.co.

30. Quoted in Gray Area, "Westend."
31. Quoted in DJ Mag, "Top 100 DJs 2024."
32. Quoted in DJ Mag, "Top 100 DJs 2024."
33. Gill, "What Is the Most Important Job of a DJ?"
34. DJ Shinski, *Day in the Life of a DJ*, YouTube, March 22, 2024. www.youtube.com/watch?v=cYQoCkmuD04.

Sound Engineer

35. Quoted in Jeremy Alves, "Nathan Bond—Alumni Spotlight," OIART, September 9, 2024. www.oiart.org.
36. Quoted in William Stokes, "Talkback: Isabel Gracefield," *Sound on Sound*, May 2021. www.soundonsound.com.
37. Quoted in What Do You Do?, *Why Being an Audio Engineer Is So Cool*, YouTube, February 1, 2023. www.youtube.com/watch?v=uOEItzAF5L8.
38. Quoted in SonicScoop, *Top 10 Reasons Not to Be an Audio Engineer*, YouTube, April 15, 2021. www.youtube.com/watch?v=MB5fOUmvsMA.
39. Quoted in Stokes, "Talkback."
40. Quoted in Stokes, "Talkback."
41. Quoted in Khan Academy, *Audio Engineer: What I Do & How Much I Make*, YouTube, March 21, 2018. www.youtube.com/watch?v=SCVNcUvRX98.
42. Quoted in Khan Academy, "Audio Engineer."
43. Quoted in What Do You Do?, *Why Being an Audio Engineer Is So Cool*.

Agents and Managers

44. Quoted in Sophie Caraan, "How Veli Went from Hoop Dreams to Managing Artists," Hypebeast, August 7, 2023. https://hypebeast.com.
45. Quoted in MusiCounts, *Track: Career Profiles—a Day in the Life of a Booking Agent with Stefanie Purificati*, YouTube, June 3, 2021. www.youtube.com/watch?v=jaUFBptd1RY.
46. Quoted in Music Forward Foundation, *Day in the Life: Artist Management—Industry Sessions*, YouTube, February 29, 2024. www.youtube.com/watch?v=Q62VG_VN3Wg.
47. Quoted in Music Forward Foundation, *Day in the Life*.
48. Quoted in Music Forward Foundation, *Day in the Life*.
49. Quoted in Music Forward Foundation, *Day in the Life*.

Interview with a DJ

Jess Morgan of Duluth, Minnesota, is a DJ known as Jesscribe the Vibe. Morgan began working as a DJ in 2016 and answered questions about her work via email.

Q: Why did you become a DJ?
A: I thought it would be a good continuation of my education as a musician. As a DJ, I could learn more about sound equipment and practice skills that were relevant to other aspects of music and performing. Being a wedding DJ or even a club DJ can be a lucrative way to continue to grow skills, see what people are excited to listen to right now, and earn some funds.

Q: How did you become a DJ?
A: After graduating with a B.A. in music from Lawrence University in 2016, I was looking around for jobs. There was a company that was teaching folks how to DJ. I took a few classes with them, shadowed as a wedding DJ, hosted trivia nights, and after about 10 wedding gigs as a shadowing DJ, I started to do DJing on my own. Working there helped me gain professional sound experience that I was then able to apply to other sound tech gigs in the area, such as at a small performing arts theater. After a few years doing sound tech gigs, I wrote a grant to purchase some of my own sound equipment. This has opened up the type of gigs that I can be contracted for, now that I have my own speakers, mixer, and microphones.

Q: What is your typical workday like when you have a DJ gig?
A: During a typical wedding, those days can be really long! You may be preparing your wedding clothes that morning, loading up your vehicle with sound equipment, and taking a long drive. For longer gigs, it's good to charge enough for a hotel stay, or to have

that worked into your contract. Early on, I'd sometimes work a 12-hour workday and drive five hours that day, too. I wouldn't recommend this. Have strong work boundaries around your expectations when you need to do a lot of driving.

[You also need to touch base] with the venue in order to set up two to three hours before the ceremony or reception. [The day also involves] running sound for the ceremony (if they want you to do both), moving the sound system for the reception, running sound then, packing up at the end of the night, and driving back. You may also need to unload gear when you return. It can be a lot of lifting!

Q: What do you like most about your job?

A: Setting my own schedule is great! Having a job where you're connecting with people through music and dancing is also really wonderful. I like that it keeps my knowledge of current music fresh. I also like that I'm able to be creative at my workplace, especially when I create my own event.

Q: What do you like least about your job?

A: Sometimes the days can be really long! If you're feeling sick that day, it can be a lot harder to call in when someone is relying on you to keep their wedding going. As a contractor, you want to have emergency back-up DJs or friends worked out. But sometimes you need to just strap in and make the event happen however you can. I've definitely DJ'd events where I've had a migraine. But this responsibility has also made me take my physical and mental health more seriously, since I need to be so "on" during big events and stay healthy for big days.

Q: What personal qualities do you find most valuable for this type of work?

A: I really love people, and I think that helps me with this type of work. Being able to really want to meet people where they're at, finding what music makes them excited. Having a good memory can also help. If you're at a regular venue, it can mean a lot to people when you remember what songs or music they requested last time when they come to the booth. It also helps to be genuinely excited about music, so that learning new tunes feels more exciting than daunting. And have patience. Sometimes people will really test you when they come to request songs or interact with you. Being confident, sure of yourself, firm and patient can all be really helpful while interacting with dancers.

Q: What advice do you have for students who might be interested in this career?

A: Learn as much as you can about sound production and sound tech companies in your area. Being on a team with other people or working for a company is often a great way to get started. It's also good to have a working MP3 file library and to keep this as organized as possible. A lot of venues have Wi-Fi, and there are DJ streaming services, but you're going to want to have back-up options, and the ability to completely DJ from MP3 files if you need to.

Other Jobs in the Music Industry

Accompanist
Band director
Chamber musician
Choral director
Choreographer
Composer
Conductor
Copyright consultant
Cruise ship entertainer
Festival manager
Forensic musicologist
Instrument repair technician
Lyricist
Music editor for films and television shows
Music festival marketer
Music lawyer
Music producer
Music professor
Music teacher
Pit orchestra musician
Radio DJ
Session musician
Singer
Songwriter
Studio manager
Theater manager
Vocal coach
Worship leader

Editor's note: The online *Occupational Outlook Handbook* of the US Department of Labor's Bureau of Labor Statistics is an excellent source of information on jobs in hundreds of career fields, including many of those listed here. The *Occupational Outlook Handbook* may be accessed online at www.bls.gov/ooh.

Index

Note: Boldface page numbers indicate illustrations.

Picture Credits

Cover: Friends Stock/Shutterstock

10: Pixel-Shot/Shutterstock
19: MindStorm/Shutterstock
32: Aleksander Kamasi/Shutterstock
42: Nomad_Soul/Shutterstock

About the Author

Terri Dougherty has written more than one hundred books for children and young adults. She loves exploring new areas and has written about a variety of topics. She lives in Appleton, Wisconsin, with her husband, Denis. They enjoy hiking, biking, and traveling, especially visiting their three grown children.